Modern Society and Oppression of Thought

by

R. J. WEKER

ISBN-10: 1981712623
ISBN-13: 978-1981712625

For more information and updates, go to:

www.RJWeker.com

TABLE OF CONTENTS

PREFACE

This book is meant to be a discussion starter. While I do not whole heatedly believe everything explained here, I do believe it is very important to have these conversations in this continually oppressed space of freedom of speech.

At this point in time, where we're beginning this century, and this millennium as a whole, the social environment of the world is changing at an unprecedented pace thanks to new technologies which push us further and further towards a true global society, and in such, a universal human culture will emerge.

So, before we proceed into the future, we must step back a moment and widen our perspective of our views on society. We need to reflect on what exactly is going on, with a large *"why?"* we never seem to ask ourselves. We get so tunneled down on current ongoings that we fail to see or understand a larger picture, which will lead us blindly into the future of the human race. If we don't know where we come from we cannot map out where we're going.

There are going to be socially unacceptable thoughts that I ask we take at least one last honest look at. And, of course, politically incorrect views not very welcome to discussion in our current close-minded "liberal" society. But I must beg of you not to make it your personal objective to mentally disprove every single line you read, keep an honest open mind. I know this is impossible, but in saying this I hope it will at least make you aware of that you're doing it.

Going on to address the other type of readers that may pick up this book: it's is meant to be a discussion starter and <u>not</u> a bible of instruction or thought. I want you to think, not to accept blindly all the arguments set fourth because you want to agree with them. If you pay attention you will even find contradictions between the chapters, that is because I want you to think carefully about the different arguments and, after careful meditation, proceed as you wish. Hopefully this book will offer every reader something to think about and everyone will be able to come off reading it with new thoughts.

1

THE PROBLEM

It seems curious sometimes how hypocrisy and cognitive dissonance take effect on even the greatest minds and the best of people. In fact it's an inherent trait of human behavioral nature: without it, almost certainly, society and civilization may not have been able to emerge. But we also posses the distinctive trait of self-awareness, and with such, the ability to recognize our own fallacies and, through reasoning, understand them; and finally with some difficulty and compromise to our self-being, confront them.

Martin Luther King, Jr. famously said: *"I have a dream that my four little children will one day live in a nation where they will not be judged by the color of their skin, but by the content of their character"*. Today, we live in a nation where this dream is much closer than ever to being fulfilled. But at the same time, as of late, things are taking a surprisingly opposite turn. In fact, looking beyond our given filters, it seems as though people are judged very much based on their color, ethnicity, background or self-identification. All that's really changed is our perception on these matters.

We glorify minorities, or the now preferred title: *victims*. And seem to have a societal hatred towards majorities. This needs to be specified a little more: what "minorities" and what "majorities"? How exactly are we judging what members pertain to these groups? It seems to me as though we're talking more about the color of their skin than that of their character. We're talking about where they fall in superficial characteristics: such as sex, race or other identifications. In doing so we're not erasing these classifications from within the human species, but we're perpetuating them. The title of being a victim or being offended or having had ancestors suffer in the past has become some sort-of reward. And this is very damaging: it does not empower them, and it forces them to think of themselves in a certain way.

It glorifies a "it's not my fault, it's because of *X*" attitude. Even if it is true, or like most cases *was* true at some past point, by glorifying victimization and the lack of fault, you impede their own self-empowerment and perpetuate the idea that they are poor victims of *X* that can't do anything.

This is not unlike a teacher telling a child that he has been brought up wrong and misbehaves because of his parents, and that that will impede his success in life. This, followed by rewarding him, either literally or through special treatment for being such a "poor helpless soul". He will go on to life, if he is not strong-spirited enough, blaming his failures on his parents or on whatever else he can. Furthermore, his mentality will be altered so as to always be fixated on his problems and misfortunes. Even when succeeding, his focus will be more so on what's going wrong than what's going well, and there will always be someone or something to blame for them. Consequently, he will live a bitter life full of self-pity, and with very little confidence of his own.

Even if what the teacher had said about his parents *was* true, if the teacher had instead given him detention for his misbehavior in class, and instead of a reward, sat down with him and told him clearly not to let where he comes from define him. Instead, to take hold of his own life, to rise above and be better and to go on to do or be whatever he wants to. By teaching the child to not let a background of family problems define him, the outcome would obviously be very different, he would find himself empowered with the choices of what he can do or be in life.

Now, to be clear, I do not mean that all the weight of the child's outcome in life would be totally dependent on this single instance, but you get what I'm saying. Over one's childhood years and growing up, we pick up how we'll see ourselves for the rest of our lives. Only with great strength and self-awareness can we later change this. Everything is down to perspective: negative people live bitter lives, because all they see is their misfortunes. The same is true for optimistic people, who despite their downfalls and failures, they will see the positive side of the situations, be generally happier and much more likely to get back up on their feet with the same, or more, confidence as before.

If we really want to make society a better place for all people we must rid ourselves of this victim culture of "nothing's our fault" and teach true empowerment, not: *"Oh, you're black – that's really going to hold you back. I'm really sorry, there really is nothing I can do. Why don't you just go on to live your life wishing you were born someone else."* And what's even worse, is going on to "be prideful" of this "condition" with others like you, creating a group mentality that serves no other purpose other than short-term reward and does nothing to solve anything.

We need to start judging on character, not on superficial traits such as color, identification and background. That just furthers their distinctions within society and proceeds to marginalizing them even more. Giving groups "special benefits and treatment" does <u>not</u> help their confidence or self-esteem. Letting minorities into higher education with lower grades because of the color of their skin is very much still racism, and what's worse: if they possess knowledge of this, that they got in just because the color of their skin or because of where their parents were born and <u>not</u> because of their actual performance or earned worth, how does that affect their self-esteem? Same goes for how Oxford allowed it's female students in STEM courses to have 15 more minutes to do their math or computer science exams.

What message is this sending? It's not one of empowerment, it's one that's quite blatantly saying: *"well, maybe you're just not as good at this than the opposite sex, but don't worry, we'll give you extra time"*. Personally, this would negatively impact my ego and I would feel either dumb or incompetent - that to yield the same results I need additional help.

What all this ends up doing is making them all classify themselves as a member of a certain group based solely on external traits – and not their character or abilities. They have no earned worth, and what's worse is that not only society sees them like this, but themselves as well. They no longer see themselves as empowered individuals who can go out and achieve big things, but as another anonymous member of an oppressed group who pat each other on the back and never really learn what they are actually capable of gong out and doing.

And what does putting people into groups in this manner actually do? Well, it certainly makes manipulating people's thinking and ideologies much easier. It eliminates the individual, with whom you no longer have to reason with. All you do is convince a single entity (the group) that "it is in their best interest" to do or think "X". And like sheep, the rest will follow.

2

MODERN OPPRESSION

The question of how the "left" oppresses the members of society and how they became so strong is the same one. The answer to both questions is by being completely intolerant. Surprising? You don't believe me? They have become very apt at social perspective manipulation and portray a large amount of cognitive dissonance, maybe not any more so than any other given human individual, but it does seem to be a little better targeted. When you hear of them what may come to mind is: a diverse, freethinking group of students of different ethnicity, sexual orientation and self-identifications. But all these traits ("diversities") are superficial at best. We, as a society, are backing into an incredibly superficial, materialistic world; no wonder Marxism and glorified communism is on the rise.

You see, what you won't find in these circles of people is true diversity of ideologies, values, morals, opinions or beliefs. And those you will find are very superficial or minor, nothing truly fundamental. Surprisingly, the "conservatives" uphold a far wider and diverse portfolio of ideas, and are much, much more tolerant of contrary opinions. How many times have you heard of a "triggered" or "offended" conservative who can't tolerate your right to freedom of speech and expression? Probably not nearly as much as the exact situation in the left.

The Evelyn Beatrice Hall quote "I disapprove of what you say, but I will defend to the death your right to say it" is often thought as a leftist idea. And throughout history it has been, up until recently, when liberalism became separated from totalitarian leftism. While "classical liberals" or what now may be deemed as modern conservatives still keep this at heart. In fact, the current "liberals" are actually fighting for the opposite. And you must see the problem here already: one group tolerates the other, but the tolerated group doesn't return the favor, and is intolerant to the other. So the group empowered by the tolerance it has from it's proclaimed enemies can easily overpower them by going against any kind of sound morals and becoming disrespectful and intolerant towards the group that does just that for them.

Restriction of freedom of speech is a very real and scary problem we're now faced with. Liberals have taken-on an almost totalitarian position on speech, thought and behavioral restriction. Ironic, as totalitarian is synonym with *illiberal: adj. 1. opposed to liberal principles; restricting freedom of thought or behavior (Oxford Dictionary)*. So if these so called "liberals" of today aren't actually liberals, what are they? It's time to take away our filters and try and see things a little better. They seem more intent on *controlling* thought and ideas, and forcing everyone to adopt their "universally true values". Personally, I'm starting to think this whole "liberal" thing is actually a facade, and they're actually more interested in power: a kind of Orwellian-power over people's thinking, even promoting mass amounts of "doublethink", or as I mentioned earlier, focusing cognitive dissonance to particular subjects.

If you look at today's universities, places where we're supposed to learn how to think freely and learn important knowledge, you'll see that already over half of them <u>do not</u> allow freedom of speech to be exercised (lest it might "offend" someone) and focus heavily on the indoctrination of their personal standpoints on the world. Many speakers have started to be disinvited based on holding an opposing view. This makes sure that even the speakers that come from outside the University fall exactly into the same set of ideas and values as the university is trying to brainwash it's students into having. I wonder what happened to the idea of seeing things from as many perspectives as possible and then being free to choose through critical thinking what seems to be the most correct or objective. And by going through this process you remain always open to new ideas, perspectives and the changing of your mind upon a better idea. And that sounds very liberal to me. You actually understand how and why you got to the final conclusion, and that it was of your choice, so you remain open to hearing more arguments, applying a little critical thinking and improving your thinking and values.

Sadly, this is the opposite of what's going on, essentially dumbing-down the population. They are given an idea and the supposed opposing one, grossly misrepresented, along with all the arguments of why the former is the correct one, and given no other choice but to accept it – lest they be the villainized "totalitarians" that uphold the opposing idea. And what's even worse is that these ideas start to trickle down into high-school, primary school and even kindergarten. And if we're raising individuals from the very start within one single line of thought _and_ depriving them of the skill of critical thinking, then we're raising a generation of pawns to an ideology, not of actual free individuals or even less so, leaders and revolutionaries. I want to clarify that I do not believe there is anything wrong with raising children with a specific set of values or under a particular type of thought. In fact it is necessary for their proper development, but we must also make sure to include in their teaching the ability of thinking critically and for oneself. As well as many ideas being portrayed going against common sense, and not only that, but shifting all the time, making it unstable, not unlike the citizens of "1984's" London.

What's almost even more worrying is that the bigger portion of all mainstream media falls into these deceptive lines of thought, aligning itself with the glorified double-think they don't even believe themselves: but perpetuate because it's taboo to say anything against it yet praised if they pretend to believe it and promote it. And going further than that, our main sources of web interaction suffer from a strong censorship few even know about. They are, after all, private platforms whose managers ideologies, or at least their concerns as to who they mustn't offend, leak down to attack differing ideas through their policies. Facebook, Twitter and Google all seem to be attacking differing ideas, through very vague "policy breaches" that don't seem to affect people who fall in line with their views.

On Twitter many conservative icons are constantly suspended, banned or restricted. The comedian/commentator Steven Crowder has recently had problems on Twitter as they banned him for a advertisement campaign *they* actually wrote for him. As well as some of his videos being pulled from YouTube almost at publication. Or PraguerU's YouTube videos that are now being classified as restricted content and their on-going legal battle against internet censorship.

Sadly, there are far too many examples and I will not go in to them. But I *will* raise the question of the morality of this happening: would it be in their right as private owners of the mediums to censor the information on their sites? Or should they be subject to some kind of responsibility with the power they hold over us? What is right and what should be done is a very complex question I wouldn't pretend to have the answer to. But what I *can* say is that we can rightfully do one thing, and that is fight. We must stand up for each-other, stand up for the diversity of ideas and have initiative of our own. While we could go as far as to create mediums of our own, that would be highly impracticable and improbable for success. And worse, it would just become another closed bubble and serve no purpose to the furthering of ourselves. But if more people were made aware and were convinced it was unjust, now that could start something. That said, it would be really tricky because people do not have in their minds anymore the tolerance or support for what they perceive as "bad ideas". Although if that were to happen, then something could change, as these are, after all, businesses who seek to accommodate the biggest group of clients as possible, or at least the most intrusive or powerful.

All of this leads up to impact freshly "educated" youths: this becoming all they've ever known and they don't question it. And slowly we all embrace the lie, again, not dissimilar to Orwell's 1984. As no one dares speak against it, and your own group of friends or family may call you out on it because it's taboo to talk on the topic anything other than positive things. And in some cases even if saying a positive thing about one of them actually doesn't make any sense when encouraging another. But a handy bit of double-think does the trick. Just pretending the problem doesn't exist will never do anything to solve it, and that's why those with the knowledge of what's actually going on should speak up.

This is how something so vague as leftist ideology can be so strong, because they don't question it at all. So with both the education systems *and* the media representing this bubble, and later-on corporate cultures are forced to start embracing these same things and we find ourselves in a very bad situation. Most of the older people don't actually believe in a lot of it, but they play along with it out of fear and oppression. And the younger generations don't know of anything else. So we have this situation which isn't viable for prosperity in the long run, and it *will* weaken and destroy our society if nothing is done about it in time. Already, nearly half of new generations favor limitation of speech, and even the banning of scientific research that may offend or go against a group of people. We're already well on our way to being a close-minded society of sheep – sheep that think they are diverse and freethinking. Progress cannot be made without conflict and different ideas, and *this* idea at least most people will agree with. *But* many people on the left practice a different idea: that only under their "perfect set of ideas" can we progress. All opposing ideas are outdated things of the past, that must be forgotten and even pretend they never existed, unless convenient to resurrect them so as to demonize them along with the group they are trying to get rid of. If we're not growing, we're dying.

This is commonly seen in a very hurtful thing going on: "justified" double-standards. The very same types of things and questionings many conservatives suffer from members of the so well-wishing left, if reversed, could land those conservatives in prison, fined, fired or at least "disgraced" in the public eye. It is the finest hypocrisy – the one that will further your monopoly on thought. The media is especially damaging as it's not an objective source of information – but carefully selected and crafted propaganda and wide-spread social manipulation.

Now, as media outlets *do* have to choose what to air, a true objective source of information will always be impossible. What I would propose would be to either diversify the thought within each outlet: to have diversity within the outlet's employees and directors. But this approach would be idealistic at best, and probably very impractical. The other solution, would be for the individual to try and take action for oneself and diversify one's media input. If enough people did this it would be able to shift and change the market, and make it a more equal playground for free thought and information. But it takes something that is sometimes hard on the modern individual: taking initiative and moving beyond consuming what's it's being force-fed.

We have all heard of the ultimate trick to hold someone captive as a prisoner is to make sure they do not know, or even question, if they are in a prison. The exact same goes with controlling what people think or believe. The modern "liberal" is praised for being "diverse", forward-thinking and a fighter for "liberal principles". But somehow, through either very clever or very dumb mechanisms, they actually go completely against the most important liberal principles: individualism, liberty, equality and pluralism. Due to misinformation and logical misguidance (hopefully – it would trouble me if they were doing it on purpose), they blindly fight against what they think they stand for.

They do not stand for individualism at all, but still claim they are against totalitarianism, which is the opposite. They act and think as a group, marching blindly to support something someone smarter has told them to fight for while unknowingly promoting more vile causes hidden within the implications of what they fight for. They love thinking as a group and creating more groups: ways to easily classify people and tell them what to think because they now belong to "X" - so they *have to* also stand for, or against, *Y & Z.* At their centers their causes are not what they advertise to be: often misleading and vague terms such as "equality for all peoples" or "justice for *X*" - and *X* being another group they created to further divide society and control with ease the individual mind. They want the world to be black and white, right or left, A or B. If everyone is forced to belong to one of two prescribed options, it's much simpler to sneak in what the people at the top want, and as A has to stand for A and be against B, they have no other option but to accept everything A promotes or *God-forbid* switch to B – which is presented as polar-opposite to themselves.

Hard work is gone into indoctrinating everyone to think the same and to think in groups. They work hard to delimitate "victims" by superficial traits such as race, ethnicity and sexual preference. Thus putting these groups in small compartments, easy to manage and manipulate, while promoting their victim-hood to "bring justice for them" while in reality it is for the reason above. They focus always on "this" group and "that" group and completely dismiss the individual, along with it's capabilities and it's ability to think, decide and even empower itself without the help of the thought-overlords.

This weakens individual thought, because even if they agree, they may only agree on 95% of everything they say but still feel forced to accept the other 5% because *"it's who I am, I must stand with my group"*. This is exactly why they dominate the scene, because scattered individuals cannot fight against a mass of dumbed-down, same-thinking people. There is no longer pluralism, but simple dualism: us and them. Liberty is repressed, you cannot exist outside of the dual-system. If you speak your mind, whatever it is, you're automatically categorized into A or B, liberal or conservative, this or that.

Even though you may personally conserve your individuality, society will automatically classify you and treat you as such. You do not have liberty in your actions or decisions either because the big groups, aided by political correctness, will cut you off and oppress you to their best ability. There are many examples, like the cases in which Christian bakers refuse to sell a wedding cake to a homosexual couple. In most of the cases the bakers were really nice about it: one even told them he would gladly make them a cake for the wedding, just not the actual wedding cake, as it goes against their personal religious beliefs. But of course, they proceeded to be outraged and sought a highly publicized campaign against them. It's curious how when researching this again it is really hard to find any news articles that don't highly condemn the bakers.

At what point does who's right trump the other's? It's a complicated question. But in practicality, we somehow know. It's the ones wielding the scissors of political correctness. Now, I'm no Christian, but I really believe they should have respected the bakers and not forced them to ascribe to what their group is fighting for "or else". There are many cases of similar situations and it is a discussion we haven't properly had yet without a strong bias one way or the other. And what actually really worries me is that I would bet that if those bakers were Muslims and not Christians, things would have been totally different.

It seems like the ideals of equality being pushed for are not between individuals, but between groups or categories of individuals. In such, a small group can face-off the largest numbered group as equals. This is promoted as a way to seek equality for all people by making easily managed groups. And it means the majority is at odds with insignificantly small groups, but must defend itself as equal in value. So the individual thinking of the masses becomes reversed to the thinking of a couple of "representatives" of each group. More than often then not, causing the majority to loose favor. So we're not fighting for the majority's well-being, but the minority's ease of gaining power and comfort. The individual cedes it's right to equality to the group. Why are we predisposed against majorities? Shouldn't we want to accommodate the greatest number of people and adopt into it those not yet accommodated? Instead of forcing the majority of people to go against their will to accommodate insignificant numbers of people?

We end up with a dumb and controllable society. And in a almost ironical sense, the marginalized "conservatives" have become the classical liberals, and are the ones upholding the diversity of ideas. This is exactly where the imbalance of power comes from. The left seeks total control and abolition of all ideas contrary to theirs, while the tolerant right tolerates their opinions, and the tolerated use this to their advantage, albeit not dissimilar to even the Church's or other ideologies' strategies throughout history, and tries to stab them in the back through the good-willingness of the tolerant. And now they have so much power they can drown out the voices they don't want heard.

The old saying: "live and let live" becomes a thing of the past, a "bad" and dangerous idea that should be more of an "accept *or else*". It's a fascist regime over thought and opinion. When is the last time you dared confront a "liberal's" opinion? And if you did, how'd that turn out for you? *"-Aren't you tolerant?"* *"-Well, yes, but you're not being very tolerant towards me right now".* Many of the people (unless living inside a bubble of their own ideas such as a Church or other group) who disapprove of abortion, or incorrect gender identifications or whatever it may be, keep it to themselves and are fearful that anyone found out. <u>This is not a freethinking society.</u> Ironically, the death of this phrase was even pointed it out by themselves, in a 2013 article published by Huffington post actually called "Live and Let Live isn't Enough Anymore". They branded the saying as being homophobic. An excerpt goes: *"[...] I realized that that is the problem. To live and let live is not enough anymore. It's no longer sufficient for our straight friends to say, "Hey, I have no problem with you being gay," [...]"* and goes on to explain what you should do instead to make sure you're not homophobic: *"You can do things as simple as donating to pro-LGBT charities, volunteering at an LGBT youth organization or voting <u>intelligently</u>!"*. I kid you not, look it up for yourself and read the article.

And they don't seem to realize that what they are doing is crushing other people's religious freedom and freedom of belief. They are actually stating that they're sure their idea is better and worth more. So much so, that you must actually abandon yours and support and preach theirs!

Give them money too, and why not vote for who they are want while you're at it? All of this while preaching the <u>equality</u> of rights, ideas, cultures, etc. There exists a significant dissonance here that should be corrected: either change your title of "liberal" to something more suiting or start respecting other people.

3
WHAT HAPPENED

What I seek to explore in this book is how our current western society shaped itself and study how we're been moving towards a universal human culture globalization. We'll see how the current most influential culture came to take over the world, and it's current problems. It is a call to action, as we enter this millennium, to seek out the best future possible for the human race at this turning point. I will to start out with a very specific and recent example and go larger and further back from there on, until we have a large enough perspective so as to address the picture as a whole.

To begin, let's look at how the victimization power game has been working, alongside skillful social marketing and public persuasion, to bring minuscule societal movements to rise to international prominence and discussion.

To best explain the mechanics in place I will look at the evolution of the gay community in the past 30 years. The movement as we know it today can be said that it started just over 30 years ago when the article *"The overhauling of straight America"* was published in the *"Guide"* magazine in 1987. Two years later, it was expanded and published as a book titled: *"After the ball: How America will conquer it's fear and hatred of gays in the 90's".* I believe this is the best demonstration of public persuasion and social marketing I can use, both because it worked great, and we have recent memory of just how it evolved. It's an excellent guide on how to shape the thinking of an entire society.

It came at a desperate time for the gay community: the height of the AIDS crisis' momentum. As the virus had started to make itself out of homosexual groups into the mainstream, they had to do something so as to not be blamed for the virus, which would mark them once again as America's untouchables. Consequently, seriously harming their efforts to become desensitized in the public eye and gain rights as legal couples. They had to act fast, and this guide proved to be the exact thing they were waiting for. And not only for them, but it proves a generally excellent guide on how any small, frowned upon group of people can rise up to great social prevalence. It was a very centralized effort for social manipulation, not only for their group, but it proved great tactics for any group seeking to do the same. Living completely in the extreme left, it gave them a great advantage as a whole: that of the overly empowered "victim".

Let's look though the original article, and feel free to look it up yourself and read though it too if you wish. We'll be replacing homosexuals with *group X* so that you're not limited in thought as to who has used these methods. The fist step fleshed out is for *group X* to achieve desensitization in the public eye: <u>1. Talk about gays and gayness as</u>

<u>loudly as possible.</u> Thirty years ago, the average citizen, let's call him *Joe*, would have been repulsed at seeing two men kissing at the park. Or even overhearing them at a coffee shop talking about gay love-life in a encouraging light (theirs or someone else's). But then Joe starts to encounter this on a more regular basis, seeing gay couples holding hands on the metro on his way back home, in line for the movie theater, or at XYZ places "talking about gays and gayness as loudly as possible". Soon, he will be tricked into accepting the agenda being pushed as "just another thing"; "normal"; and, inflating the size of the group, as "everywhere". He will likely come up with self-persuading thoughts like "I guess times change". In this first step, *group X* must also start trying to make itself into the media.

Closely following the first step is the one of aggressively taking on the role of victims. Victims who need protection, this will trigger Joe's instincts to assume the role of protector of the less fortunate. Here is where we already start to encounter the power game, Joe now will start to feel a little empowered as said "protector". But the power actually lies with the said "victim". The article expresses the importance of pushing a week and defenseless image of their group, stating to: "avoid jaunty mustached musclemen in gay commercials, so as to emphasize more good-natured attractive people to further the image of defenseless victims". And an excerpt of the article goes: *"gays must be cast as victims in need of protection [...] if gays are presented, instead, as a strong and prideful tribe promoting a rigidly nonconformist and deviant lifestyle, they are more likely to be seen as a public menace that justifies resistance and oppression".*

At this point in the article it stresses the importance of emphasizing two essential messages. The first, and most important, is that they must present themselves as victims of fate. This will mean that they have no other option or solution to the nature of their being, presenting it as being a natural occurrence. It instructs they must use this message: *"As far as gays can tell, they were born gay, just as you were born heterosexual or white or black or bright or athletic. Nobody ever tricked or seduced them; they never made a choice, and are not morally blameworthy. What they do isn't willfully contrary – it's only natural for them. This twist of fate could have easily have happened to you!".* It again states the importance of having in their campaigns very decent and unexceptional characters, indistinguishable by all normal standards, appealing and admirable. The *"Joes"* must not be given the chance to use excuses like "they are not like us". The advertisements have to transmit the message of: *"these folks are victims of a fate that could have happened to me".*

These claims were completely unfounded by the way: even now there's still not sure cause. Scientists have discovered some genetic links, but mostly they're environmental causes, and if there are environmental causes it means it is not something you're just born with. Like the studies on identical twins showing that if one twin turns out to be homosexual the possibility of the other also being gay hovers only around 10%, while if it were genetic it would be a 100%. Many have stated it was in fact their choice, many of these same ones than received backlash from gay communities. This seems to suggest, as with most mental illnesses, that it is a question of a complex inter-relation of the factors present. That is also my stance on the matter, there can be no arguing it is a mental illness. Animals, as we are, have two sole instincts that drives their existence: survive and reproduce. And we as mammals have a male-female reproductive system. Due to our overly sized brains and having already dominated (in the modern world) our need for instinctual survival through civilization, it leaves us with only the instinct of reproducing. But through socio-cultural re-wiring of the brain due to how we're changed our social environment in this immense complex system our brains have created society and life as a human to be, our brains started changing the concept of mere simple reproduction to a romanticized and invented concept, we cannot seem to properly understand or explain, known as "love". Through transcending our basic instincts, we needed to keep our brains working at something, and this was meant to drive us to reproduce and grow families in more efficient ways for being able to pass the enormous amount of information needed to navigate what human society has become. But doing what we're best at: inventing abstract concepts, this one soon became detached from it's purpose, becoming something "more" and allowed for people to start "falling in love" with members of their own sex. I do not mean to say what they feel isn't legitimate, just that sexual attraction and love in general for humans it is not what many think it to be. You cannot say someone with Major Depression doesn't legitimately feel depressed, or someone with Schizophrenia isn't legitimately hallucinating. Looking at mental illness in animals, we find that it is extremely uncommon compared to humans. Simple forms of mental illness such as PTSD, Anxiety and OCD (simple because of clear effects and causes) can be found, but are almost exclusive to domestic or captive animals. This shows that metal illness seems to be a side effect of human societal structure, and that would also explain the incredible rise of mental illness in the last decades as life becomes "easier", more abstract and more interconnected. We've never had such "freedom" as beings, but we've never felt so trapped either.

Going back to the article, the second of the two messages to be transmitted is a simple yet very effective one. They must make public as many stories and images of *group X* being brutalized, and, quote: *"dramatizations of job and housing insecurity, loss of child custody, public humiliation [...]"*. Now, while I do acknowledge they have suffered a lot as a group, I don't think it has been so noteworthy in the scale of human suffering to justify how they've convinced the remaining 90% of their neighbors that they are terrible human beings filled with hatred and disregard for "love" if they do not wholeheartedly support and promote this small group of people to their best effort. What this caused was a strong shift in powers as the larger part of the population becomes the oppressed for not sharing the same views as whatever *group X* is pushing. And as time goes on, in an increasingly privatized manner, until diverging views become obsolete from the public sphere, and thus, eventually dead. But, as they do remain a smaller portion of society, and with the erratic mentality that "a minority cannot oppress a majority" (apparently ignoring millennia of richer people controlling the masses, or even our smaller countries oppressing much larger 3rd world countries), they remain with the much sought-after title of "victims" and the rest, as the heartless oppressors.

There is far worse suffering in the world, affecting greater numbers of people, and even in our own countries there are the forgotten groups lacking the privilege this group had to project themselves as these victims in need of protection. After being bullied you can still go home to a warm bed, after having had a hot shower, to tweet about your oppression on phones assembled using materials extracted by children in mines, by other hard suffering groups. Human suffering is hard to measure, but it seems that the "worst" of it (or at least the one "currently" the most worth fighting for) is always the highest publicized, backed by gain for one group or another. I do not mean to disregard their suffering, but I wanted to point out that they have been more privileged than they think, and to scale human suffering for wider perspectives as we go on to the next chapters.

The third point outlined in the article, is the very clever one of giving the so-called "protectors" a cause bigger than *"group X"*, one they can relate to and fight for. Examples would be *freedom of speech*, *freedom of beliefs* and *equal rights*. That creates a very clever game, as with these concepts it becomes very hard to draw "fair" lines within, which has caused many ethical debates ever since their very conception. That is due to their nature of being human inventions. For if "A" believes "B" to be a violation of it's rights, but "B" believes "A" infringe on it's rights, who is right and who deserves to become the "intolerant" and have their rights "corrected"? Who will the scissors of political correctness prey at? (Or any sort of right restricting mechanism) Well, easy, it depends on who's wielding them as our "just" commander. You see what happens? These concepts sound great but fail miserably in the real world, and sadly, I do not believe there is any objectively fair solution readily available.

Continuing to the end of the main objectives in the article, we find two simple and well tested methods you've probably used yourself in your daily life. The first is: <u>4. Make gays look good</u>, an old and easy trick, used most predominately through sentences like: "Did you know [insert important, famous or relevant name here] was "*X*"?" Be it about a particular ethnicity, religion or even geographical location (such as your hometown, state or country), we've all heard something like this. And I do not mean to say t is always for social marketing, we as humans treasure particular nuggets of information such as these, especially if they can allow us to feel proud about something.

This uses the "exception proves the rule" fallacy. I'll elaborate: by overexposing the exceptions, people eventually can be tricked into thinking that these exceptions <u>are</u> the rule. Such as "artists are usually gay" (calling someone "arty" or "artistic" is sometimes even used as an euphemism for being homosexual), and many racial stereotypes go this way as well. But don't be tricked, in many of these instances those are the exceptions, and that is what makes them notable of mentioning. They are the unusual cases, that prove the rule, but if you go around parroting all the exceptions, you eventually forget about the majority of cases. This is of course just one part of this point of making the members of *group X* look good.

Naturally, the next point is the exact reverse: <u>5. Make the victimizers look bad.</u> And it feeds directly off of the fallacy explained above. Here the article contains this quote: *"... we intend to make the anti-gays look so nasty that average Americans will want to disassociate themselves from such types."* A harsh statement, but if you think about it, it worked marvelously. It specifies in the article to use images of Nazi concentration camps where gays were tortured and gassed, convicts talking about the "fags" they have killed or would like to kill, the KKK expressing their hatred for them, and *"bigoted southern ministers drooling with hysterical hatred to a degree that looks both comical and deranged".*

These, are of course exceptions in our society (e.g. Christians <u>do not</u> hate the gays, in fact, it would be a sin for them to do so. Years of image abuse using the most extreme cases has really damaged their image on many fronts). But the fallacy worked great, and poor average Joe had little intention of being associated with "such types".

After this, the article goes on to describe exactly how to perform, over a stretched amount of time, a series of excellently crafted commercials and other public relationship strategies. The two writers were, after all, honor students from Harvard, very prolific in psychology, social science and marketing. Hunter Madsen has an impressive career in marketing, having worked with many large brands and was even one of the pioneers of the beginning of internet advertising. This ending part of the original article contains a elaborate 4-part campaign with detailed advertising examples and formats starting very subtly and slowly rising in exposure. It also calls for funds to fund such a campaign so as to out-buy their rivals. And it ends with the call to action that if they do not act now, and aggressively fight for a very favorable image, they would forever be blamed for the AIDS epidemic, and return to be detested untouchables.

I thoroughly recommend that you do an internet search for this original article *("The Overhauling of Straight America")* and read through it, it's posted in it's entirety for free on a couple sites. This would assure you I am not quoting anything out of context or cherry-picking. And I believe it's important to understand where and current dominating social movements come from, and why and how they rise above others.

I want to make clear that I am not at all saying this article invented the game or started it, but it does a good job at concreting the methods. Having been written 30 years ago, and working to near perfection, we can read it while having the last three decades as example to see how exactly it played out. And lastly, this will allow you to gain a basic understanding of the rules of this "game". You'll be surprised at how many, now and throughout history, have used similar methods of social manipulation to get what they wanted, and oppress those they didn't want heard. Most notably going back all the way back to how Machiavelli's "The Prince" instructs 16th century leaders on how to gain and maintain social favor.

And now, due to what will explain in the following chapters, practically any of us can play successfully. In the article replace "gays" with whatever you want and you'll see how current emerging groups are still using these same techniques. Maybe you'll even want to give it a shot yourself, or fight back a little fairer, now having the basics to get started.

Notes on current societal groups:

It's curious how there is always a pendulum movement within culture, one way than the other, always reaching new extremes. This is exactly how and why cultures keep changing and evolving, it's never stable or simply stopped, always swinging left and right.

Right now, it's swinging very far up the left spectrum. All of it's components are inter-connecting, eliminating the various levels one could stand within to form a strong and consistent block. Like how the gay movement eventually evolving into LGBT+, tricking people simply attracted to the same sex into forcefully having to stand-up for and support people suffering from severe identity disorders (transgenders, people who even invent their own "identities", etc) and other things as well. If you remember back enough, when they started out they avoided associating themselves with those groups too extreme. But these later-added groups used the same system to gain entry into the first one. And after gaining access to piggybacking off the first, they Trojan-horsed themselves into mainstream culture.

Eventually other groups like third-wave feminism, BLM, and others started making themselves into the mix by "standing up for each other" as the "oppressed" collective. In some cases damaging their original intent for the sake of the new collective, like how current feminists only seem to care about women who share the same opinions as their side of the spectrum. I know many women opposing their views who are continually harassed by these "feminists". They don't stand for women anymore, they stand for the ideas they want to push, and in such failing to represent women as a whole.

This new collective used the tactics described previously and managed to convince the media and the public eye through aggressive "Make the victimizers look bad" [Step 5 in the article], that opposers were indeed "evil". Thus forcing "Joe" not to want any type of association with the opposition, leaving him instead with no other option but to support the new mild to extreme left conglomerate. If he doesn't he will be branded as a fascist, homophobic, white supremacist Nazi, who doesn't deserve to have his rights or his say in anything or he should kill himself. I'm almost positive you have heard harassment of this type before, for example saying something against the fat-positiveness movement such as: you think it's a very unhealthy trail of thought to teach people to actually want to be unhealthy, and then proceed to be screamed at as a "f**king Nazi" or similar. It wouldn't be a first for me.

One recent example of this kind of harassment is the recent case that went viral of a porn star who committed suicide. She refused to do a porn scene with a male counterpart who also did gay porn scenes, for fear of having a higher risk of contracting a STD. This caused a massive backlash as she was quickly branded as homophobic (which she wasn't, and has even done many lesbian scenes and has never spoken out against the gay community, she was just afraid of getting a STD from performing with a higher-risk individual with no available tests). Some comments on her twitter said she should either kill herself or apologize. Two days later she hanged herself. Of course she was already a vulnerable person suffering from depression and bipolar disorder, but the fast mountain of hate she suddenly received is what pushed herself to do it.

What happened is that the left, through the vigorous association between all it's components, made of it a solid and consistent group. This causes it to augment in strength and size, and in doing so, pulling the balance strongly towards it's side and causing the other side to compress it's diversity into a small segment on this line. That damages the conservative side, the public eye places all of it's different groups very close to each other, from most mild to most extreme. Even though within they remain very segmented: a regular church-going or mosque-going family is put into the same tiny room as the most extreme of groups from Neo-Nazi white supremacists to Islamic terrorists. These average families feel very asphyxiated in this position as they don't want anything to do with those extreme groups, but at the same time, they don't want to be forced to go against everything they believe in by shifting to the other side, so they either lose their freedom of belief, or their freedom of speech. Most of the times they feel very oppressed in speaking out, so they don't, and it causes them to become obsolete, as the groups who are barking loudly take center stage. And they become just part of the mass slowly being dragged by gravity towards the most prominent side. That causes the problem that if these poor oppressed souls eventually have to accept and support "W", they become forced to also include X, Y & Z. All this because of their fear of being misclassified by the left's manipulation of the public eye.

This is very wrongful and oppressing to the major portion of the population that resides in the middle grounds and to the people on the right. They are inflicted with fear of speaking out their values and even political views, and in doing so, they lose their right to do so. Not in a legal way, but caused by mass social bulling, they are oppressed into restraining from using their right. This causes that only the people at the most extreme side of the right spectrum speak out, contributing to the illusion of the right the left is pushing.

So, what can you do? Use their game and let your voice be heard. Hopefully many will realize how much they've oppressed the rest of us. Speak your mind, and make sure the message of you supporting X, doesn't necessarily mean you support Y&Z. Even if you are homosexual or supportive of the homosexual movement, and for example don't support transgenders, let your voice be heard. Although I have to admit, you will find very few sympathizers at first in doing this. We must break re-grow the diversity of thought and relearn critical thinking to regain balance. Reach a point where both sides can understand the other and stop oppressing contrary ideas.

MORAL ORIGINS

So what shaped society to be able to work in the ways I described in the previous chapter? It's curious how smaller groups in society with no tangible (traditional) power such as command over armed forces or wealth can rise to such culture-shaping power. The reason is Christianity and "white people's culture", the second of which I will discuss in the third chapter. Think a little way back to fundamentals of modern democracy and civilization: America's Constitution and Bill of Rights. This became a prototype for the foundation documents of all modern democracies (of course they are many other, older examples, but I suspect this to be one of the most known and cited ones). The document was based on the intoxicating idea that everyone is created equal before the eyes of God. That, by the way, also implies that there would be more to us as individuals than our physical bodies.

This dangerous idea intoxicated the greatest empire of all time, the Roman empire. The greatest not because of size and or power (even though it did have a fair share), but because of it's influence that eventually reached every single nation on earth; it's even still doing so now, over a millennia and a half later. This simple idea, originating from a small group of Jews in a corner of the empire managed to spread throughout the reaches of the empire in a matter of just a few centuries. And eventually, come the age of Imperialism, to all the other continents. Later on it was further cemented into the world through globalism and thanks to the world wars at the beginning of the 20th century it became an international staple through the United Nations with their acclaimed universal human rights.

Animals do not have equal rights. For any species other than ourselves, it's the survival of the fittest. If you are born smaller, weaker, sickly, less aggressive, dumber or disabled in any way your chances of survival are slimmer than your counterparts. Let alone your chances of prosperity within a social group if we're talking about a social animal. That means you are by no means equal in any way to your fellows. Sure, you pertain to the same species, but what does that mean? A weak runt isn't seen by the others the same way as the strongest of the pack.

It was the same with humans until, through the cognitive revolution, we started creating "imagined powers" that gave us more attributes other than just our physical selves. Things like the concept of propriety or "power" assigned from a "higher power" that says I should rule over you. These ideas & religions usually stayed pretty limited to their associated cultures. Their followers in most cases didn't even believe they were assignable to others: the "magic tree" of the valley our tribe lives in isn't preaching about a universal message for all people, and the existence of our neighbors' "magic river" doesn't in any way disprove our god. This made, in some cases, compatibility between different peoples merging. A good example would be how the polytheism of India, in a variety of cases, was easily able to accept the conquering people's god simply as another valid option, and not at all invalidating to their existing ones. Even within the polytheistic Roman and Greek cultures, when conquering new regions such as Egypt, many of the gods were able to cross cultures.

When monotheism first emerged with the Jewish culture, *they* were God's chosen people. Their message had nothing to offer to anyone else. This incompatibility caused a problem for them, as they refused to accept other idols, while at the same time their title of "God's chosen people" was exclusive to them. The rulers of the land didn't always find that to be of their liking, causing a lot of oppression and a very bloody history with other cultures. For most of history there never was a concept of equality, there was always the conquerors and the conquered. And the latter was never on par with the former.

The Romans started to revolutionize this a little with the Roman citizenship they started offering to free males within their empire (the Greeks did have citizenship as well, but it limited to each city-state, and never for it's conquered people). This was a big step forward towards how we understand modern civilizations to be. But it was lacking backing from a "higher-power" like I explained earlier to really make it something truly transcendent, something that would last even after the fall of it's structure. It needed something truly remarkable and larger than anything ever seen before.

This is when the concept of a universal religion, a single all-powerful God for every human being on Earth, struck through the Empire. It was exactly what it needed to rise to be the most influential culture ever to roam the globe. It created the building blocks for almost every way the world *thinks* today. The marrying of the ideas already within the Greco-Roman culture, such as citizenship becoming a political attribute more than an ethnic one (many people throughout Europe, even after the fall of the Roman empire still called themselves "Romans"). And things like politics, philosophy, art, literature, architecture, strategy, etc. Combined with Christianity's morals, values and most importantly the idea of tolerance (as we all are equal under the eyes of God), created a base "universal" culture that was able to take over the whole world.

This was largely because all of these are notions that are independent from the distinct nations and states, making them invulnerable to their rises and demises. In fact, they continue to spread today through globalization. For good commercial trading and international relations, less influential countries find themselves imposed with this western culture consisting of both our political and economic systems, and later of our values of equality, freedom and human rights. Slowly they go succeeding, first through political and economic adjustments, and later and slower to our values and thinking. These contagious thoughts appeal to the masses, lesser than the more fortunate above them. And our western influence over these other nations also fills our want to "help one another as equals", while giving us deep-down the tingling sense of superiority and empowerment we love so much.

The social power game eventually became a more subtle art. Now ruled by the infamous political correctness, which does more harm than good. You're not even "allowed" to "offend" anyone, which I personally don't understand why we have gone so far to worry so much about everyone's "feelings" like children. It's ridiculous people have even gotten so feeble-minded, and it continues to do so as mental illness is at an <u>all-time</u> high. Majoritarian thought and ideas become equal in value as minoritarian ideas, and furthermore, as any thought out there. Causing a sense of disequilibrium: repressing the majorities as those contrary take their power and through carefully crafted technique, command.

The problem with equality of thought, speech and equal rights (I do not mean strictly as *legal* rights) is that they are impossible. There will always be conflict, people pro-X and against X cannot both win. This works on many scales, from macro scales like Christianity and Islam both wanting to convert all the non-believers: including each-other. To pro-life, pro-choice like situations. Pro-lifers believe in the unalienable right to life, so pro-choice supporters deprive in their eyes the most fundamental right a human has. It's not a question of them just not doing it and the other group doing so, it's a question of their very own culture's laws going against a firm belief of theirs. This alienates the entire group from feeling fully identified with the constitutions of their society. It doesn't work for any of the parties without imposing one of the groups values onto the other. So you either brainwash the whole population to think the same and lose our freedom of thought, or one group comes out unhappy. The trick both groups use here is the timeless trick of placing a fictitious higher-power to back to their argument. In this case arguing for a human right. But it can never work properly, as they are imagined.

It seems as though the losing side will, for the most part, always contain the majority of people. Or at least always contain the previous dominating majority, as with time the new generations enter into the emerging line of thought. These new lines of thought emerge small, and game themselves up in power, eventually overthrowing the majority, and then the majority has to follow suit to avoid being branded as backward-thinking, and the new generations are brainwashed into the new ruling order. As the known quote goes: *"To learn who rules over you, simply find out who you are not allowed to criticize"* (Quote often missattributed to Voltaire on the internet, due to the original author's dark history). You'll see that this quote applies perfectly to this power game of political correctness and victimization. The minoritarian X groups are pretty much untouchable as far as negative critique in mainstream media and social environments such as work or school. You can go to will loose your job for so-called "hate speech". And are publicly condemned if you speak out your beliefs and they are contrary to what the left is currently pushing. It's curious how it's okay to offend and speak out against Christians but not Muslims. Christians are constantly bashed by the left for opposing homosexuality, but they defend Muslims, who also, and more fervently oppose homosexuality. How is it fair that you can offend and insult Christians in the same way the left holds itself so sensitive to "emotional damage" and "oppression"?

As I said before, this balance causes in a great number of people oppression and fear of speaking out, causing those who do to appear prominent and twists your perception of who is actually majority. *"The smallest dog barks the loudest"*, and in the globalized world, if you actually look at the numbers as a whole: that dog is very, very small. America is a mere 4% of the global population, and these groups are minorities within this population. Yet they are shaping the future at an incredibly fast pace, because nobody is speaking out, and those who do are few and quickly branded as haters and outcast.

WHITE CULTURE

I could have used "western culture", but in light of the rising hate towards "white people" I wanted to point out that the western culture *is* white culture: the culture originating from the Greco-Roman meets Jewish-sect culture. And by an immense difference, the dominating one. Although curious enough, as described earlier, the white race *is* a minority in the global scale. Similar to what I previously discussed, this minority has easily ruled the world for more than many centuries. Be it directly, or indirectly via it's influence. But the white race it seems is meeting it's demise in the public eye, again, curiously in it's largest inhabited countries. Why is this? Well, it's because the white culture grew separate from the white race (similar to the Roman citizenship separating itself from the original "Romans"). And it grew so much it expanded to the dominating heights of the globe, spreading across, at this point, to pretty much all countries it's democracy, human rights, it's institutions and even it's inventions (such as electricity, cars, airplanes, internet, computers and so on). The globalizing of the culture, now appropriated by pretty much all other races exposes the white race as a no-longer necessary "dominating majority" or oppressor.

Using the fallacy of the whites being majority and the victim-oppressor game, a white male is now the absolute least of things to be proud of. And as those in power write history, the white race becomes the blame for all the pain in this world and the "evilest of evils". Using the same exact techniques I have already described, white people are now associated with Nazis, slavers, white supremacists, bigots, etc. And sure, we have done evil. But may I ask the question if this is a race exclusive? Throughout the history of humans there has always been very vile acts, on all fronts, but the winners always point the blame in the opposite direction of themselves. And even though most do know they did things of equal cruelty, they are more or less happy to ignore it and enjoy being on the winning side.

For example, there is now in America a big amount of racism towards white people because of slavery. But it's curious how this is an idea the Greco-Roman culture borrowed from the ancient civilizations of the Middle-East and Africa. And after the Roman Empire fell, in the Medieval Age of Christian Europe it had practically disappeared (or taken-on a new form: serfdom with the feudal system). It lingered longer in the countries linked to the Arab world, culture where it continued to flourish.

In the rest of the world slavery continued untouched by the white culture's values. It was only when Europeans started branching out into the world again that it became prominent in our culture. The "New World" provided a plethora of new goods that the European citizen would now be able to afford, as the countries got richer. But these goods required a large amount of man-power to harvest and work in the fields, so slavery started coming back thanks to human greed. Curiously slavery wasn't nearly as big in North America as South America and the Caribbean, but to the public eye it seems like America was by far the worst, and even sometimes the one responsible for slavery. The new-found western slavery didn't last very long. What we think-of when we hear "slavery" today rose and fell in just over 200 years. It was unsustainable to our universalist values and morals. And was nothing compared to how long it had existed in other cultures.

In fact, people seem to forget that slavery is a bigger problem today than in all the rest of history. There are far more slaves today than at any other given point in time. But no one cares, because it's Blacks owned by Blacks or Asians owned by Asians in 3rd world countries. It doesn't fit anyone's agenda in the western world. Well, except for white culture as a whole - still fighting for international laws regarding this by elevating more countries into the global network we are becoming. I have never heard anyone blame black people or any other race for what's going on. Why? Because it has nothing to do with race. It is a cultural thing. And all the races living in western countries now pertain to the western culture, where they blame the members of the original race of the culture for how they were first treated. They are the ones that make it racial, because they don't want it to be a cultural thing, because it would point back to *their* culture.

Now in our culture everyone can prosper. I'm sure many people will say otherwise and claim that racism still makes it much harder for some. I will not deny this claim, it's true. So why is that? Because of a failure in cultural adjustment. Incoming cultures are encouraged to cultural diversity, lessening the effects of the larger local culture (again through the effects described formerly). As an example, why is the African-American sub-culture so crime-ridden? You probably don't know the numbers because they're taboo. In the US in 2015, 229 black people were killed by white people. Meanwhile 500 white people were killed by black people. The difference is about double. But only if the country's distribution were 50-50, if you consider white people consist of 77.1% of the population, while African-originating people are only 13.3% (also 2015 figures) you see just how big of a difference there really is. Think about it. But the biggest problem is: (in 2017's consensus) white citizens killed 2,574 white people. And black citizens killed 2,380 black people. You may think the numbers are pretty close, but you must take in consideration again that black citizens consist of only 13.3% of the population, that makes these figures a little worrying. They are also the majority of victims, at 52% of all victims. I do not believe this to be due to race at all, but to culture, and in this case, a sub-culture. The fault lies in both sides, it's the failure of merging into a single homogeneous society. Whites reject this sub-culture marginalizing them to to see no other option but to stick to the street culture they have. But at the same time, through their culture they reject ours, such as sticking to music about problems they can relate to, which in turn brainwashes them to continue living these problems. The cultures never merged completely and remain separate, because we see cultural diversity as a good thing. But it is not, it divides us.

The white culture has given the world everything that makes it run today. From the organizational structures of state and thought like democracy, modern politics, modern economics, philosophy, values... To all major modern inventions, science and medicine. Just think: from motors (steam, combustion *and* electric) to electricity itself. Light bulbs, computers, software, internet, cars, planes, motor boats, etc. Meanwhile people living in totally alienated cultures (such as tribes in Africa, South America and Oceania) still live in the stone age. They haven't even invented the wheel yet, or even reached the bronze-age. As they haven't even invented written language, they're stuck in prehistory. But we have already flown out into space and navigated the depths of the ocean with submarines. We have technology like GPS systems to map the entire world, they barely have seen the neighboring regions. This is due to the differences in the culture's fundamentals, theirs doesn't call for them to do any of these.

The average IQ levels in sub-Saharan nations are about the same as what in the western world we would classify as mild mental retardation (they hover around 60 points, mild mental retardation is between 50-55 to 70). While our societal systems have became so complex they have elevated ours to above 95 points, and in south-east Asia to 105 points. Our world is so much more complex than theirs. I do not mean to say they have less potential as fellow humans, if you get a child just born in one of these countries and drop him in a western middle-class home he will easily be able to go on and succeed in the globalized world. But the same goes for the reverse. It's all down to different human cultures.

That is one of the reasons why the refugee crisis in Europe has been so dangerous, because they haven't been culturally trained into our system before arriving. And added to the current games in place, such as political correctness and cultural forgiveness they prosper and disrupt. Why isn't the enormous rape crisis on mainstream media? Germany is aggressively hiding the actual numbers and forcing the media to omit crimes by refugees so as to maintain a politically correct stance on mass immigration. In 2015, migrants committed 1,683 sex crimes, in the last three-quarters of 2016, the number rose to 2,790. That's around 10 instances every single day. In official reports they have omit the term "migrants" so people don't see the scale of the problem and panic. Instead they use terms like southern-looking and other terms so all the reports don't contain the same words. According to André Schulz, head of the Association of Criminal Police in 2014, up to 90% the sex crimes don't appear in the official statistics. And according to the minister of Justice, Heiko Maas, only 1 in 10 rapes are reported, and of these only 8% result in convictions (meaning that less than 1% of rapists are actually ever convicted). This is largely due to "cultural forgiveness" to their culture, arguments like "they don't know any better". Well may I ask: why don't we make them know better? They should receive cultural training in a separate location first, and have the second-generations released into the country, after going through our educational system. This may seem like brainwashing, that's because it is. But it's necessary if we want to continue to prosper at our current rate and make the world what we see as a better place.

On a more positive note, it may seem like the world is getting worse day by day, but it's not. In fact, thanks to the globalization of white culture, the world as a whole has never in history been a more peaceful and safe place. More people have rights than ever before, crime is lower than the news may make you think, and our life expectancy is only rising thanks to advancements in modern medicine.

But back to the negative, the problem in Europe has spread so badly there have even been instances of woman being warned by the police to try not to dress lightly in the months of summer, as it could trigger a sexual assault. You see what happens here? Her rights are being oppressed, and she doesn't become the victim, but the provoker. The crime becomes her fault for being "insensitive" because "they don't know any better". But again, shouldn't we make sure they know better before entering the country? They even started affecting local traditions, as they are branded Un-Islamic and very offensive to their culture (such as alcohol consumption at Oktoberfest, which attendance dropped to a 15-year low due to fears of sex crimes by the thousands of refugees arriving in Munich). As I explained in the previous chapter, I do not believe equal rights, as we idealistically see them, are possible.

Shifting to problems in the US, we find a fast rise of hatred towards white people. And the problem is that it is not considered politically incorrect, racist or even hate speech. In fact, politically correctness often finds itself encouraging it and surely does not find it wrong. Many "X" groups back this movement as well, and curiously most left-wing "X" groups are the "whitest" thing to have happened to the country. White people who aren't a part of these liberal circles are starting to become a little hopeless in the face of this hate and degenerative comments such as "check your privilege, f*cking cis white male" and other hate speech they don't consider hate speech. But if it's not, than what is it?

At the beginning of 2017 four black youths tortured a mentally disabled white 18 year-old while live streaming the video on Facebook while saying things like "f*ck white people". At the time of me writing this only one of them has gone through trial. She was given 4 years of probation and 200 hours community service – for torturing and scarring for life a poor disabled kid. Then they complain when people are a little reserved towards them in fear. I have no doubt he will be left with a poor image of people of their color, especially because they were doing it as race hate crime, evident because of their statements. But another hate crime was committed recently as well, a Florida man broke into a mosque, smashed the windows and lights and left a slab of bacon. He was sentenced to 15 years of prison and 15 more of probation. Sure, that was really wrong of him. But how did he get 15 years prison for "offending" people and someone who actually physically tortured, as well as verbally abusing another human because of the color of his skin get only 200 hours of community work? The Florida Muslim-hater didn't scar anyone for life. I am not defending this in the least, just pointing out unbalance in the justice system. Why exactly did these two trials play out this way? *"The intent is to really deter similar kinds of hate crime"* said the Imam who oversees the network of mosques in that area. And sure, I agree, Islamophobia is on the rise, and this harsh punishment will deter similar crimes (another similar case from 2016 only got 12 months).

So how come was there a heated debate as to whether the torture video was even a hate crime or not? To see the bias just invert the races of the people in the video, if it were white people torturing a defenseless black special-needs kid while stating "f*ck black people" it would have blown-up and their punishment would have definitely been more severe.

In short, don't be fooled by hatred towards white people. The white race has shaped the world as we know it, and despite all the scary news going around, the world really is a better place than it's ever been. In the western world slavery isn't a mainstream problem anymore either, so don't let yourself be tricked into thinking we were the bad ones that started it. We actually were the ones to end it. And now thanks to our prosperity, other countries are starting to accept human rights and eventually, equal human rights. And we aren't exclusive either, as we spread and share our culture and inventions, and accept anyone to be a part of our culture. You may be thinking: *"yeah, by destroying and ruining all the other cultures"*, if you are, then "check your privilege", as they say, next time you go to vote, turn on an electric light, watch a video on YouTube, go to the cinema, or travel by plane. Or would you rather be stuck in the stone age? Or if you're a woman, live in Saudi Arabia where you're not allowed to even go anywhere without a male guardian or covering your hair? All the people speaking against this "white privilege" are *living in* "white privilege" and, independently of their race, pertain to white culture.

 6
MEN & FEMINISM

Going down the list of things political correctness represses me from talking about, I thought, after hearing degenerative comments towards "white men", and already having covered "white" - I should cover "men" as well.

An interesting quote I heard was: *"every single society was built on the disposability of it's sons (men)"*. Modern feminists seem to believe their life has always been of "lesser value" than of men. But ever since I was born, reality has been different. "Men must protect women" seems to be saying that as women are lesser, so men must protect them. That is what I thought too, but in reality, what that statement manipulates the male gender role to be is that the man's job is to suffer, endure and be disposable for the females' sake. A man is a admired if he sacrifices his life for his country, wife and children. He mustn't mind taking all the hard, labor-intensive jobs so his wife and kids can have a good life – to allow his wife to give their kids a good future, while he is absent, working as a dehumanized provider. He is meant to be a disposable and replaceable source of production and protection.

Woman say they are seen as sex objects, but men are seen as success objects. We are forced into the belief that if we aren't successful at providing for "the lesser" around us, we are useless. A man who cannot provide for himself and his family is no man. Meanwhile, a woman doesn't have this stigma; she isn't seen as lesser if she isn't providing the major part of income; and if she does achieve any level of success, she is highly praised; while men are just told their penis did it for them and can do better, receiving little to no support.

The real problem is that today's gender roles are diversifying. Or better said, the female gender role is. They are no longer seen as just means of reproduction, and are free to do whatever they want. In fact, men enrolled in collage are now a minority, and the majority of dropouts in both high-school and collage are males. Someone has to do the dirty jobs, and no one seems to care about the back-end of what it takes to keep our civilization running.

We have advanced to a point we don't even realize that the paper you are reading this on was a tree; a tree men had to go cut down in the forests of the Amazon, not an easy task, then transport it to a facility, trim it, shave it, cut it, and so on. Or the trucks that carried it are built of metals, metals that have to be mined in extreme conditions. Same goes for the material that makes up your house or whatever building you may find yourself in, or the tarmac that constitutes the roads. Or all the work it takes to build and construct these. And what of agriculture and farming? Or military drafting to defend the country? If you go up the Empire State building in

New York and look around at the enormous city before you, ask yourself, how much of this did men build? Not only the construction, but the mining, extraction and processing of the raw materials to form everything you see. Not only buildings, but cars, boats and planes. Even all the lights you see if you go up at night, they are mostly powered by coal, that has to be extracted as well. How many of those men do you think worked those horrible jobs, giving them chronic health problems and slashing their life expectancy, in order to selflessly provide for their families? Do you really think they worked those jobs to feel empowered over their wives? They did it to act as some kind of working machine, sacrificing time with their families to provide a source of survival, and if they were lucky enough, means so that their kids can have a better fate.

In traditional gender roles, the male is to be the the means of production, and the women the source of reproduction. Our two most basic instincts: survive and replace. Now the female role has is changing, but not the male's. Men increasingly have the worst cut of the deal, but because of our unchanging gender role we have keep our heads down, keep providing and supporting the women's decisions. For many years it has been illegal to pay differently for the same job based on gender (or race, or anything else). Men tend to aim for the higher paying jobs because of the need of proving ourselves as success objects.

And while this is now changing in the high-up "good" positions, there has been absolutely no change to all the men-dominated baseline jobs. I have never heard anyone protesting unfair gender distribution in the mines, construction sites or male drafting. That's because it remains the man's job to defend and produce for society. Even today, in major accidents such as planes and boats crashing, it's still women and children first. Children for an obvious reason, and women because the role of the mother is far more valuable than that of the father. The father is absent and at work, a replaceable means of production. A woman can always find support and help in the case of things going badly south. A man, no so easily, because he is seen to have failed his role in society. It's no wonder the majority of homeless are male. A woman can find support much easier, and even when they are homeless they get accepted into shelters much more readily. And then if they were to need to find a job they easily are provided with career training, a foot in the door and good references. But men are put on a list of 50-100 other men for low-paying labor intensive jobs, and treated more infra-human than as actual people. If they cannot cope; they are easy to replace. And the jobs remain at long hours and low-paying wages because of this fact. They become entrapped in a circle.

Likewise, woman have many more rights than men. Not as prominently in legal terms as in social terms. A female allegation against a man is taken as a fact, every single time. A woman may be beating a man, and if she somehow gets hurt in the process, or he so much as breaks her fingernail chances are he'll be on his way to prison shortly. There are even terrible cases of men accused falsely of paternity, and the mother can take legal measures stop you from being able to take a DNA test, forcing an innocent individual to have to pay child support.

Child support itself, how many times has it ruined the life of a man? And why is it practically always the man's job to *provide* and the woman to raise the child? Here we see those exact gender roles in play. Such is what happened to Frank Serpico; the hero that unveiled corruption within the NYPD, was tricked into having a child with a woman he was seeing. The woman allegedly told a friend her plan, meaning that it had been totally intentional by her part; fact that won her the case in court. And so, Serpico after retiring a hero and even having been shot (there is a film about is time at the NYPD), was to pay half of his well-earned police pension to that woman.

In 2014, according to the Federal office of Child Support Enforcement, only 5% of mothers pay child support;compared to a whopping 85% of fathers. And in certain cases, even if the father has custody of the Child, he may still have to pay support if he earns more money, but never in reverse. This becomes even worse if the child isn't even yours, but she claims it is. Men are simply disposable providers.

The expectations on men are very high. They must be strong, successful, stand up for others, etc. "A man has to do what a man has to do". In the original Forced Labor Convention, which was founded to fight slavery, states in article 11 that forced labor *may* be imposed on "adult able-bodied males between the ages of 18 and 45". The so-called patriarchy feminists regard as the problem is merely the result of gender roles, not the cause of them. It's men falling into their expected role, or they are "good for nothings".

It's increasingly getting worse to be a male as well, there is a very strong feminist movement supported my many, but every men's rights movement is labeled misogynistic, fascist, evil, woman-hating, etc. And for sure they do attract people of those descriptions, and fail to attract the standard Joe because of that game in play and these associated labels. This is merely an illusion, they have good causes and good ideas. But they are being crushed in the public eye.

You cannot only change one of the two fundamental roles, by doing so you will hurt the other side.

The things those groups fight for are things like: males being the majority of the homeless & the great majority of suicides – 4 out of 5 (if you're arguing every point I spell out, now will probably come to your mind: *"But women attempt suicide more times than men, so: ha! I caught you".* If that's the case you better check what you value and how you think. You are disregarding the <u>*actual lost lives*</u> of these people so as to give the same credit to failed attempts *just because of their sex*). Other male-dominating things are drug users, the unemployed, school drop-outs and prisoners. Prisoners who, by the way, serve 63% more jail time for the same crimes as females; who are as well as twice as likely to avoid incarceration if convicted. The judges' leniency towards them is justified for "practical" reasons such as: *"women have greater care-taking responsibilities".* If you agree with this, than you have to admit as a society we value their lives and their freedom more because of their traditional gender role. Men aren't seen as the warmhearted care-taker, it's better if he's in jail over the mother. Men aren't even seen as good single parents. I know of some incredible warmhearted fathers, but as a society we just don't give them a chance, and having these roles don't help. If you had to choose which parent in a traditional family consisting of a husband & wife with three children - without knowing anything else about them - had to be shipped away and cast into slavery, who would you instinctively choose?

Back into the list of male "privileges", we also find that men are more unlikely to look after themselves; they consist of almost all the victims of Autism Spectrum Disorder; are more prone to dying from cancer (207.9 of every 100,000 men versus 145.4 of every 100,000 women); and consist of *93% of all work-place fatalities*. Why then is there such large campaigns for breast cancer, but hardly ever any cancer campaigns targeted at male victims? Men are even very seldomly accepted into abuse shelters, and in most cases forced into keeping quiet.

War deaths are just beyond measure. In the Korean war 36,572 men died alongside 2 women. In Vietnam it was 58,217 males and only 8 women. The number is so large you stop caring, but can't help feeling a little sorry for those poor women. It's like filling up the Chicago Bulls' United Center <u>three times</u> with men, adding in 2 or 3 women in each iteration, and killing everyone inside. The men become these disposable entities, lacking in humanity. They are sent to be disposed of, at their expense, for the rest of us. And sure, we then build them statues, write them in the history books and give them medals and "honors"; but it has become more like the payment for their disposability.

One thing that gets me is that we always see women as more vulnerable to crime. But the reality is that men have always been the majority of victims in all forms of violent crime with the exception of rape. The latter being the least common "violent crime" and "serious intimate partner violence" being the least common of the "serious violent crimes" (Criminal Victimization, 2016 - Bureau of Justice Statistics). If you're a desperate individual on the streets, or even just trouble-makers that go around at night beating people up for the fun of it, you're much less probable to assault a female than a male. It's seen as more evil. You'll hear many of these types stating they wouldn't hit a woman, even some who've murdered in cold blood. That's because we value the lives of each sex differently.

And movements such as the pro-choice movement are pro-choice only if you're the woman. Once the child is conceived, the man has no say. If it is born against his will, he will still be forced to provide. But if it was his will for it to live, he has no say either. I've seen many cases of both. Very recently in fact, a friend of mine had an accidental pregnancy. He was actually really exited about it; they had been together for just over three years; she had moved with him from her country, where he met her while studying abroad; and he intended to keep the baby and marry her. And the plan went forward, until about a week left for her to legally be able to abort, when she panicked, flew back to her country and had the abortion. You can just imagine in what a horrible state he was left in, it was truly a terrible sight, he was totally heartbroken, he felt like he had lost his baby. And if you think men don't feel emotions you're very, very wrong about that. I often find them very sensitive, that is why they feel like they must hide this "vulnerability". By her last-minute reaction, the fact that she had a lot of problems of her own already and that this was not the first time for this to happen in her life, it probably worked out better than not for my friend. But his rapid plummet from the star-eyed excitement of *"I'm going to be a Dad! I have a baby!"* to the miserable state of depression I found him in of having lost his baby was heart-breaking.

Unknowingly, men have become the true victims of the so-called gender roles. And they're continually forced into their spots and denied the right to speak out, instructed to just keep on providing and sacrificing. And as unfair as it may seem, there may not be much point in actually speaking out because there may not be any solution at all. There are key biological differences that created these roles. Woman can give birth, which makes her a fragile liability while pregnant if working in labor intensive jobs. And men have more muscle-mass, are stronger and better fitted for labor. That is how and why society shaped itself in this way over the entire course of history. Now we're challenging this as our society started evolving at an unprecedented speed. But we're only challenging the easy part of it, and the rest remains the same, or worse.

Now, with this chapter I do not mean to say women have had it easy or haven't suffered immensely. But what I do mean to say is that everyone suffers, and it in itself is a very subjective matter very hard quantify. Arguments as to who has had to endure the worst of things are pointless, these things impossible to determine without subjectiveness, and it is the same subjectiveness of the nature of suffering that makes it indispensable in it's measuring. This being the case I suggest we abandon this competition and try to listen to both sides without trying to undermine the other. Feminism had it's good points, and still has a fair few worth looking at. But as I have said before, you cannot just change one side without he other falling terribly out of balance. The same as with humans and nature, you cannot elevate human society with our needs of building cities, roads and massive facilities to keep us afoot without the other side suffering a significant blow. I can only hope that the battle in this chapter is not as lost as the one in the example. Maybe new technologies will be able to lead the way. We seem to be reaching a future where labor-intensive jobs and defense jobs become automated, and whether we like the idea or not, this would give the two genders a fairer playing field in our slavery to the human system.

7
FINAL THOUGHTS

When we start to realize just how arbitrary human thinking really is, we can't help but be struck with pessimistic nihilism. The very things that mean the most to us don't actually "mean" anything. Morals, values and ethics don't have any kind of backing from any "higher-power", money doesn't actually mean anything, it has no "real" value, even the concept of owning something is just our invention, our treasured rights are absolutely meaningless and mostly arbitrary. "Right" and "wrong" aren't real. But yet they are. They may not be innate, "special" or noteworthy, even sometimes not even logical. But in reality they are the most powerful thing we have. They have the power of faith, your neighbor believes them, your friends, your enemy, in fact, the majority of people believe in them. And there lies their power, they allow us a system in which to work together as a collective. They are what made us go from wild animals to a tribe, from that tribe we became a city, and that city grew into a state and eventually became a nation. And through even more time, we have made ourselves become "human". A single entity, albeit not a single culture – yet; but most of us do believe that just being born comes with a set of "human" attributes or rights, the most commonly agreed on is the "right to life".

As this new millennia goes on we will become a people, as a whole (or bring ourselves to destruction), which will allow us to make our way out into the solar system and beyond. And there's a curious thing that happens: as we grow in number, one would think we would grow more diverse, but what happens is the opposite. Similar to mixing flower and milk into a consistent mix: complexity will increase to a peak and then back down once the mix is properly stirred. When it is in the process of mixing it becomes a complicated mix of flour, clumps of flour and milk; all at various stages and in different states. You can't take any given part of the mix and have it be identical to the any other part until the mix is complete. The same I see with humans: we went from a relatively organized small group of mammals to spread out into the world and diversify. We became an experiment where many different groups of isolated communities could grow and evolve and test different structures and ideas until a couple of them started taking on a strong lead. Now these have grown so strong we start to experience fast decay of diversity as we're finished being stirred into the homogeneous mix.

As we rub shoulders with more and more peoples the need for better collaboration rises. To remain functional as a large group we evolve towards thinking as a unit. And we will eventually, unless we've destroyed ourselves in the process, become a single culture. We may be put back centuries depending on how this century plays out, but if we continue surviving and growing so effectively, it is inevitable. Even those so intent on keeping their own traditions are unknowingly giving in and adopting more and more of what will become in the future the "Human Culture".

That is exactly why cultural supremacy is so important. And that is exactly why I write this book, at the turn of the millennium it is now essential that we proceed with more wisdom and caution. We are reaching the make-it or break-it point for our species, and either we will unite completely or we'll bring ourselves to an end. While some have the power to wipe out the entire human race, there are still humans living almost exactly as if they were found 30.000 years ago, kept in little protected human zoos.

Those of course are the most extreme cases, but what's not extreme and is slightly worrying is: with our uniting of the human race, larger in number people than us that hold much less progress-minded cultures than ourselves enter the playing field. Countries where women don't have rights, places where there still exists a castes system within society, groups who want systems such as sharia law implemented, and so on. This could compromise the progress of the human species.

And it shouldn't be a problem for our culture our institutions and our aim towards progress. But yet our culture has been infected from within, and I fear a regressing of a couple hundred years, or the dissolving of the current dominating culture as a whole. Here is where we must do something larger-than-ourselves and look for the "greater good" future. The best configuration. A strong species ready to reach Type I civilization (on the Kardashevk scale). Yet now as we finish merging with more populous populations behind in their social progress, through the new "liberalism" of western society their culture and views become of equal value in terms of ideas, behaviors and culture. We mustn't let this go as far as to regress us and stunt the species' growth.

Yet we must also be very weary of divisions and wars. Our society is already looking towards expanding into space, yet we still have so many problems down here. We aren't ready, even though some think we should just go for it, and that will force us to adjust accordingly. When self-driving cars came out they forced us to question our ethics and laws. How will space laws be? Who will have leverage up there? Corporations or states? Will they be new nations or extensions of our own ones? Who owns unclaimed propriety and who regulates it? We'll have to invent a plethora of new systems, and we're arguably absolutely excellent at adapting. Yet, as always, our old sense of ethics which both binds us together but slows us down as a whole questions if we even should. Like how in 2015, after discovering evidence of liquid water on Mars the Outer Space Treaty from 1967 banned the rovers from investigating. And of course there is sense in this, but at the same time, we do want to go over there ourselves, which would cause even greater harm to any possible ecosystems in place, if any.

I am in the highly unpopular opinion that we shouldn't care about anything but ourselves and our future. Because if we don't, no one else will. Every other species' survival instincts play out in this manner. If we *do* meet extraterrestrials, I doubt they would have such kind morals as we do. Life has a sole purpose: to **grow**; often broken down into the simpler biological concepts of: survive and reproduce, yet "to grow" means so much more.

But, sure, we do have powers beyond imagining above all other known species. So in the little morality with which I remain: I can agree with the illogical assumption that this gives us a certain responsibility, as God told Adam in the book of Genesis, to watch over this world. I can agree that we must do what we can, but without letting it stop us or hold us back. Once we leave Earth we could turn it into a preserve. Once we finish refining growing meat and organs from stem cells, we will be able to stop our so-called industrialized animal cruelty necessary to support such a large collective, granting us an unprecedented new level of sustainability. Where we will no longer need to bring animals with us into the Space for sustenance, but we can grow in the comfort of our own homes all the meat we need in any variety we want, even new ones. And we can have organ replacements custom-grown for us, even better than our given ones.

So, with the greater good in mind, I say we must proceed. So how do we define the greater good? For us: easy, what will allow us to grow in the most effective way possible while remaining psychologically healthy and allowing us a generally happy and comfortable living. Not as mindless farm animals, but as a collective of united individuals looking towards the future.

What of the greater good for all other life? Do what we can for our "morally" imposed responsibility. This is in reality us thinking ourselves gods to feel good about ourselves. The notion of us as responsible guardians makes us feel empowered and superior by helping out the lesser fortunate. But why not? It is much better for us to continue with our happy notions of who we are than to eradicate our morals, which would collapse society.

We must unite and form one. We may very well reach our godly selves if we don't mess up at this crucial point and unite into the strongest universal human culture possible. So for now, we continue the oldest battle known to civilization: cultural supremacy. The current extreme liberals are doing an excellent job of shaping culture. But at the same time, they contain too many fallacies and inconsistencies and are weakening the dominating culture. We must learn from them and do better at shaping the human species' future. If you look at history, it may seem like the liberals have always won, from the French Revolution or the Women's rights movement. This is a semi-fallacy. The most inclusive movement has always won, as we grow towards that single unified culture.

And there lies the problem with the current liberal movement, it is looking to include the tiniest portions of society, at the cost of the larger majorities. On a global scale, it is no longer the most inclusive: it excludes a great number of people who have very diverging views. If it were seeking to brainwash those it wouldn't be so feeble, but it seeks cultural diversity and equality for the other cultures, all while attacking it's own.

As larger groups from the rest of the world come into play, they will influence us, this is inevitable. But I'm worried we will no longer distinguish the best of the aspects and incorporate those, but also accept the worst. We should create the foundations for the future universal human culture with wisdom, not with compassion. Some time ago, if you immigrated to America, you became an American and embraced American culture. That is what made it such a destination and such a power. Yet now, you should "keep your culture" and disregard the one of the county you moved to, and even fight for it to be more inclusive to you.

People fighting for cultural diversity and against cultural appropriation are not only fighting a wrong cause, but a futile fight as well. Cultural singularity is inevitable, so what they are doing is making sure it will not be ours. And ours has become much less inclusive to others then they think, with our extreme notions on certain topics highly unwelcome to other societies. We make the others not want to join, making us not that inclusive on a global scale to larger societal groups. They fear the contamination of theirs with these things so ludicrous and radical, that ours loses it's value as the most sought-after.

What will happen if this continues is one of two things: either these thoughts will manage to make themselves eventually into Africa, China, Saudi Arabia and India; or the more probable of the two: these societies will grow in power and from stronger links between each other giving way to a new superior culture, of which we will be outcast. And as we become one people, it will be very different than what we sought, and for our current minds in our current society, a regress into the past, and a possible hazardous situation for wars.

So here lies my call to action: we must rise above and think for the future. We must think of people as a whole and proceed knowingly to the best of futures possible. We must be wary of international conflict, but also of conflict within that will weaken us to extinction. Working together, we need to consistently create the best we can be as a unit, as a species. We need to both realize the arbitrarily of morality and ethics and belief, but <u>not</u> disregard them, for they are the only thing that can bind us together. They may be imagined, but they remain the most important quality and strength of the Homo Sapiens.

ABOUT THE AUTHOR

R. J. Weker was born and raised in Europe and currently resides in the United States.

R. J. Weker is a pseudonym.

For updates and more information you can visit:

www.RJWeker.com